What do you ...
strawberries try to g...
together?
Strawberry jam.

What's red outside, pink inside and very
crowded?
A bus full of strawberry blancmange.

The
Pink and Wobbly
Joke Book

Straw Berry

Illustrated by Tony Blundell

MAMMOTH

First published in Great Britain 1990
by Mammoth
an imprint of Reed Consumer Books Ltd
Michelin House, 81 Fulham Road, London SW3 6RB
and Auckland, Melbourne, Singapore and Toronto

Reprinted 1990 (three times), 1991 (three times), 1992 (twice)

Text copyright © Martyn Forrester 1990
Illustrations copyright © Tony Blundell 1990

ISBN 0 7497 0181 1

A CIP catalogue record for this title is available
from the British Library

Photoset by Rowland Phototypesetting Ltd,
Bury St Edmunds, Suffolk

Printed in Great Britain
by Cox & Wyman Ltd, Reading, Berkshire

What's got twenty-two legs and goes "Slurp, slurp, slurp"?
A football team eating strawberry blancmange.

What's pink and wobbly and indestructible?
The Six Million Dollar Strawberry Blancmange.

What's bright blue and wobbly?
A bowl of strawberry blancmange holding its breath.

What's pink and wobbly and heavy?
*Strawberry blancmange made with
cement.*

What's grey, weighs four tons, and
leaves footprints in the strawberry
blancmange?
An elephant in the fridge.

What did the strawberry blancmange
say to the elephant?
*Nothing – strawberry blancmange can't
talk.*

What's pink and wobbly and comes
from Mars?
A Martian mallow.

What's pink and wobbly and fights
crime?
Super Blancmange.

What's green and wobbly?
A bowl of seasick blancmange.

What do you do with a bowl of blue
strawberry blancmange?
Try to cheer it up.

What's pink and goes "Wobble, wobble, bang"?
A bowl of strawberry blancmange in a minefield.

What's pink and wobbly and goes up and down twenty times a day?
A bowl of strawberry blancmange doing press-ups.

What's pink and wobbly and hangs out your underpants?
Your mum.

What's pink and wobbly and belongs to grandad?
Grandma.

What's pink and wobbly and goes
"ABC . . . slurp . . . DEF . . .
slurp"?
Grandma eating alphabet soup.

What's pink and wobbly and grows
under your nose?
Tulips.

What's small, pink and eats cakes?
A pink dwarf cake-eater.

What's pink and white, comes out
at night, and sings in a high voice?
Falsetto teeth.

What's green and wobbly and plays
rock music?
Electric catarrh.

What's green and wobbly and hangs
from trees?
Giraffe snot.

What's pink and wobbly and jumps
up and down?
*A bowl of strawberry blancmange at a
discotheque.*

What is as big as a bowl of strawberry blancmange and weighs nothing?
A bowl of strawberry blancmange's shadow.

What's pink and wobbly and travels at 110mph?
A turbo-charged bowl of strawberry blancmange.

What's pink and wobbly and green?
A bowl of strawberry blancmange with a runny nose.

What's pink and wobbly and green and brown?
A bowl of strawberry blancmange with a runny nose in a muddy field.

What's pink and wobbly, sits in the fridge and is highly dangerous?
A bowl of strawberry blancmange with a machine gun.

What's pink and wobbly and sits in the corner?
A naughty bowl of strawberry blancmange.

What's pink and wobbly, with red spots?
A bowl of strawberry blancmange with measles.

What's pink and wobbly and has a trunk?
A bowl of strawberry blancmange going on holiday.

What's pink and wobbly and swims
under the sea?
*A bowl of strawberry blancmange with an
aqualung.*

What's pink and wobbly and
noisy?
*A bowl of strawberry blancmange
with a set of drums.*

What's red and runs at 100mph?
A bionic nose.

What's red, round and cheeky?
Tomato sauce.

What's red and gives you the pips?
A telephone box.

What's red, hunted and blows up
buildings?
Guy Fox.

What's red, spreads and shouldn't
be broken?
A rash promise.

What's red and squashy and says "Pardon"?
A polite strawberry with hiccups.

What's pink and wobbly and can't stand still?
A pig in a tumble drier.

What's red and white and full of policemen?
A sunburnt Panda.

What would you get if all the cars in Britain were red?
A red carnation.

Why is getting up at five o'clock in the morning like a pig's tail?
Because it's twirly.

What do you give a sick pig?
Oinkment.

What do you call pigs who live together?
Pen friends.

16

PUPIL: Can you spell blind pig?
TEACHER: B-l-i-n-d p-i-g.
PUPIL: Wrong, it's b-l-n-d p-g. With two i's he wouldn't be blind.

DINER: Waiter, this meat isn't fit for a pig.
WAITER: I'll take it back, sir, and bring you some that is.

What does a pig use to write his letters with?
Pen and oink.

Who led 10,000 pigs up a hill and back down again?
The Grand Old Duke of Pork.

What do you call a pig thief?
A hamburglar.

Where do rich pigs live in America?
In a sty scraper.

Why is a leg of pork like an old radio?
Because both of them have a lot of crackling.

What happened to the piglet who studied Shakespeare?
He ended up in Hamlet.

What do you call a pig running around with no clothes on?
Streaky bacon.

What do you get if you cross a pig with a drummer?
Ham rolls.

What would happen if pigs could fly?
Bacon would go up.

Why should you never tell a secret to a pig?
Because they're all squealers.

What's pink and wobbly and plays football?
Queen's Pork Rangers.

What do you call it when pigs do their laundry?
Hogwash.

What do you get if you cross a pig with a young goat?
A dirty kid.

How do you take a sick pig to hospital?
In a hambulance.

Why didn't the piglets listen to their grandfather?
Because he was an old boar.

Why does a baby pig eat so much?
To make a hog of itself.

What did one pig say to the other pig?
"Let's be pen pals."

What do you get if you cross a pig with a flea?
Pork scratchings.

What is a pig's favourite ballet?
Swine Lake.

Why is the pig one of the unluckiest
animals in the farmyard?
Because it is killed before it is cured.

What do you get if you cross the M1
with a pig?
A roadhog.

How is a pig like a horse?
*When a pig is hungry it eats like a
horse, and when a horse is hungry
it eats like a pig.*

How did Mighty Pig explain his
success as an actor?
"I ham what I ham."

What's green and wobbly?
A seasick pig.

What is pigskin for?
Holding a pig together.

What kind of ties do pigs wear?
Pig sties.

Why did Cinderella's fairy godmother turn a pumpkin into a coach?
She didn't have a strawberry handy.

Why did the policeman arrest the strawberry?
It was involved in a garden plot.

How do you work out the colour of
a strawberry?
With a green gauge.

Why did the strawberry plant cry?
Because everyone was picking on it.

TEACHER: If I cut two strawberries
and two apples into ten pieces each,
what will I get?
PUPIL: A fruit salad.

Why did the baby strawberry cry?
Because his mother was in a jam.

What do farmers do to endangered
strawberries?
Put them in preserves.

Did you hear the story about the
world's biggest strawberry?
Never mind, it's over your head.

How can you tell that strawberries are lazy?
They spend their entire lives in beds.

What's red and juicy with special powers?
The Six Million Dollar Strawberry.

What's red and juicy, costs a fortune, and has her own TV programme?
The Bionic Strawberry.

What's red and juicy
and goes round
and round?
*A strawberry
in a spin-drier.*

What's red and juicy and wears sunglasses?
A strawberry on holiday.

What did the strawberry say to the hungry maggot?
"You're boring me."

What did the strawberry say to the greenfly?
"You really bug me."

What do you have when two thousand strawberries try to get through a door together?
Strawberry jam.

If a strawberry hits a peach in the mouth, what is it?
A fruit punch.

Why is a strawberry a good museum keeper?
Strawberry preserves.

Why didn't the strawberry snore?
Because it was afraid of waking up everyone else in the bed.

Why did the raspberry jelly wobble?
Because it saw the strawberry milk-shake.

What's red and points north?
A magnetic strawberry.

What's red and points south?
A stupid magnetic strawberry.

Why did the strawberry go out with
the prune?
Because he couldn't find a date.

What's red and goes up and down?
A strawberry in a lift.

What's enormous and red and says
"Fe-fi-fo-fum"?
A giant strawberry.

What's red, wears a cape, and fights crime?
Superstrawberry.

What's red and goes click-click?
A ball-point strawberry.

What's pink and wobbly and wears dark glasses?
A bowl of strawberry blancmange in disguise.

What happened to the man who couldn't tell putty from strawberry blancmange?
His windows fell out.

What's red outside, pink inside, and
very crowded?
A bus full of strawberry blancmange.

What's pink and wobbly and comes
at you from all sides?
*Stereophonic strawberry
blancmange.*

What's pink and highly
dangerous?
*Shark-infested strawberry
blancmange.*

Why did the man have to go to hospital after the strawberry blancmange fell on his head?
It was in a tin.

What's pink and stupid?
Thick strawberry blancmange.

Why do elephants paint their toe-nails pink?
So they can hide upside down in strawberry blancmange.

What's pink and highly
dangerous?
Kamikaze strawberry blancmange.

If you have a referee in boxing, a
referee in football, and a referee in
rugby, what do you have in bowls?
Strawberry blancmange.

How can you tell when there's an elephant in your strawberry blancmange?
When it's especially lumpy.

What's pink and wobbly and has four wheels?
A bowl of strawberry blancmange on a skateboard.

What's pink and wobbly and has eight wheels?
A bowl of strawberry blancmange on roller skates.

What's pink and wobbly inside and white outside?
A strawberry blancmange sandwich.

What's pink and wobbly and croaks?
A bowl of strawberry blancmange with a cold.

Why don't strawberries play football?
Have you ever seen a strawberry wearing football boots?

What's pink and wobbly and shocking?
Electric strawberry blancmange.

What do you get if you cross a sheep, a dog and a bowl of strawberry blancmange?
Collie-wobbles.

How can you tell a strawberry from an elephant?
A strawberry always forgets.

Why do strawberries always forget?
What have they got to remember?

How do you keep a strawberry from ripening in August?
Pick it in July.

When does a strawberry wear a yellow shirt?
When its red one is in the laundry.

What's red and juicy and goes round and round?
A long-playing strawberry.

What do you call a two ton strawberry with a nasty temper?
Sir!

What do lady strawberries wear for tights?
Garden hose.

What's pink and wobbly and goes round and round?
A bowl of blancmange in a revolving door.

CUSTOMER: Why has my bowl of pink blancmange got footprints in it?
WAITER: Well, you said "Fetch me a bowl of pink blancmange, and step on it."

What's pink and wobbly on top, has four legs and a tail, and whinnies?
A bowl of blancmange on a horse.

What is the best thing to put into
strawberry pie?
Your teeth!

How can you tell a strawberry from
an aspirin?
Strawberries don't come in bottles.

Why don't strawberries have
dandruff?
Did you ever see a strawberry with hair?

What's red, washable, dries quickly
and needs no ironing?
A drip-dry strawberry.

What's red and goes at 60mph?
A strawberry on a motorbike.

What's red and comes off the ground
at 200mph?
A jet-propelled strawberry.

What's red and grows in an apple tree?
A stupid strawberry.

How do you stop a herd of
strawberries from charging?
Take away their credit cards.

What's red and goes "Beep! Beep!"?
A strawberry in a traffic jam.

What is red and highly dangerous?
A herd of stampeding strawberries.

Where was the first strawberry found?
In a strawberry bed.

What's big and red and lives in Scotland?
The Loch Ness Strawberry.

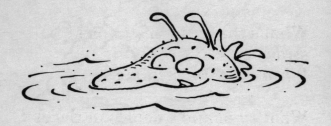

What's red and good at sums?
A strawberry with a calculator.

What's red and 440 metres high?
The Empire State Strawberry.

What's red and wears a mask?
The Lone Strawberry.

What's the best time to pick
strawberries?
When the farmer is asleep.

What's red and wobbles in the sky?
A jelly-copter.

What's red and wobbles, and fights
crime?
Jelly Savalas.

How do you start a jelly race?
Say: "Get set."

What's red and wobbles in a pram?
A jelly-baby.

What do jelly-babies wear on their feet?
Gum-boots.

What's red and wobbles in the corner of your living room?
Jelly-vision.

What's red and wobbles on the top of
spongecake and custard in the middle
of Paris?
The Trifle Tower.

"Waiter, what's the meaning of this
dead fly in my strawberry
blancmange?"
"I don't know sir, I don't tell
fortunes."

"Waiter, waiter, there's a fly in my
strawberry blancmange!"
"Would you prefer it to be served
separately?"

"Waiter, waiter, there's a fly in my
strawberry blancmange!"
"Yes sir, the chef used to be a tailor."

How many cabbages can you put in an empty sack?
One – after that, the sack isn't empty.

Why didn't the boy eat his spinach after his mother told him it would put colour in his cheeks?
He didn't want green cheeks.

What do you call a vegetable's wages?
His celery.

Why did the farmer run a steamroller over his potato patch?
Because he wanted mashed potatoes.

TEACHER (on school dinner duty): Any complaints?
PUPIL: Yes sir, these peas are too hard.
TEACHER (taking a spoonful and tasting them): They seem soft enough to me.
PUPIL: They are now. I've been chewing them for the last half hour.

CUSTOMER: Have you got any asparagus?
WAITER: No, we don't serve sparrows, and my name is *not* Gus.

What is the poorest plant?
A vine, because it cannot support itself.

What's green, lives in a pod, and is a Kung Fu expert?
Bruce Pea.

What do you get if you cross rabbits with leeks?
Bunions.

How do you make jumping beans?
Get some beans, go up behind them, and shout "Boo!"

What do you call two turnips who fall in love?
Swedehearts.

What is green, curly, and religious?
Lettuce pray.

Why was the farmer cross?
Because someone trod on his corn.

Knock, knock.
– Who's there?
Artichoke.
– Artichoke who?
Artichoke when he swallowed
strawberry blancmange.

Knock, knock.
– Who's there?
Worzel.
– Worzel who?
It's upstairs – first on the left.

Knock, knock.
– Who's there?
Beets.
– Beets who?
Beets me, but I just forgot the joke.

Knock, knock.
– Who's there?
Turnip.
– Turnip who?
Turnip for work at nine or you're fired!

Knock, knock.
– Who's there?
Lettuce.
– Lettuce who?
Lettuce tell you a few good pink and wobbly jokes!

Knock, knock.
– Who's there?
Bean.
– Bean who?
Bean working hard lately.

What is a mushroom?
A place where Eskimoes train their huskies.

Which town makes terrible sandwiches?
Oldham.

What's the best thing to eat with a jacket potato?
Button mushrooms.

Knock, knock.
– Who's there?
Strawberry.
– Strawberry who?
Knock, knock.
– Who's there?
Strawberry.
Strawberry who?

What's white on the outside and tells terrible jokes?
A corny beef sandwich.

Knock, knock.
– Who's there?
Orange.
Orange who?
Orange you glad I didn't say strawberry!

Why do toadstools grow close
together?
Because they don't need mushroom.

What's white on the outside and
acts badly?
A ham sandwich.

What's white outside, grey and slimy inside, and moves very slowly?
A slug sandwich.

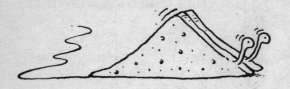

What's white on the outside, pink inside, and talks to itself?
A tongue sandwich.

What's white on the outside, grey inside, and heavy on your stomach?
An elephant sandwich.

What grows in gardens, makes a sandwich, and is dangerous if you run into it?
A hambush.

What's pink and fills policemen's sandwiches?
Truncheon meat.

What's white on the outside and scares easily?
A chicken sandwich.

What's the best way to start a pudding race?
Sago.

What's 300 metres tall, weighs 7,620 tonnes, and is made of jelly?
The Trifle Tower.

What do you call a three-barrelled rifle?
A trifle.

What's the difference between
frogspawn and tapioca pudding?
Not a lot.

How do you make an apple crumble?
Tell it that its pet hamster has just died.

Why is a cottage like meals eaten on a
sea crossing?
Two down, two up.

What's got four legs, glasses and is good
for indigestion?
The Two Rennies.

What's the best way of stopping
sea sickness?
Bolt your food down.

Why don't the Chinese eat custard?
*Have you ever tried eating custard with
chopsticks?*

What's a sick joke?
*Something that shouldn't be
brought up in conversation.*

What's yellow and smells of
bananas?
Monkey sick.

"Doctor, doctor, my tongue is as
yellow as custard, my legs feel like
jelly."
"Don't worry, you're just a trifle
ill."

What kind of salad speaks for
itself?
Tongue salad.

"What's the difference between a five pound note and a lettuce?"
"I don't know."
"You couldn't lend me a lettuce, could you?"

What did the mayonnaise say to the fridge?
"Shut the door, I'm dressing."

What's green and served hot from the oven?
An Irish salad.

What did the tomato say to the cucumber under the mistletoe?
"Lettuce alone."

How do you know a sausage doesn't like being fried?
Because it spits.

What came after the Stone Age and
the Bronze Age?
The Saus-Age.

The sausage is a cunning bird
With feathers long and wavy;
It swims about the frying pan
And makes its nest in gravy.

What car is like a sausage?
An old banger.

How do you make a sausage roll?
Push it.

What's blue and chewed by whales?
Blubber gum.

What's huge, icy and tastes delicious?
A glacier mint.

A girl in a sweetshop is one and a half metres tall and wears size four shoes. What does she weigh?
Sweets.

What happened to the man who dreamed he was eating a giant marshmallow?
He woke up to find his pillow had disappeared.

What mint can't be eaten?
The Royal Mint.

What's round, tasty and lifts weights?
An extra strong mint.

What do ghosts chew?
Booble gum.

What do you get if you cross
bubblegum with a yo-yo?
*I don't know, but if you swallow it
by mistake it comes back up.*

"Doctor, doctor, my brother thinks
he's a piece of chewing gum."
"Well send him to see me."
"I can't, he's stuck under the
table."

What's JR's favourite sweet?
Ewing gum.

What sweets do idiots like best?
Wally mixtures.

Who was the Wild West sheriff who
lived on pickled onions?
Wyatt Burp.

What's white, round and giggles?
A tickled onion.

What's white, round and jumps
around the garden?
A spring onion.

What's green, spicy and pecks trees?
Woody Woodpickle.

What's a hedgehog's favourite lunch?
Prickled onions.

What's green, sour and cleans teeth?
A tooth pickle.

What's green, wears a black cloak and
holds up stage coaches?
Dick Gherkin.

What did the cucumber say to the jam
jar?
*"If you'd kept your mouth shut I wouldn't
be in this pickle."*

"Doctor, doctor, for the last ten years
my brother has believed he is a hen."
"Goodness gracious, why didn't you
come to me sooner?"
"We needed the eggs."

"Doctor, doctor, my mother thinks I'm crazy because I prefer pink socks to grey ones."
"What's crazy about that? So do I."
"Really? How do you like them — fried or boiled?"

"Doctor, doctor, I feel like a strawberry."
"So do I — get me one too."

"Doctor, doctor, this banana diet isn't working on me."
"Stop scratching and come down from the curtains."

"Doctor, doctor, can you give me something for my liver?"
"How about a pound of onions?"

Doctor: I'm afraid you've only got three minutes to live.
Patient: Is there nothing you can do for me?
Doctor: I could boil you an egg . . .

"Doctor, my family think I'm mad."
"Why?"
"Because I like sausages."
"Nonsense, I like sausages too."
"You do? You must come round and see my collection. I've got hundreds."

"Doctor, doctor, I keep thinking I'm a strawberry."
"Hmmm. You're really in a jam, aren't you?"

A man went to the doctor complaining he was not feeling very well. "What do you eat?" the doctor asked. "I eat only snooker balls," came the reply. "Snooker balls?" "Yes, I have yellow and red balls for breakfast, black and brown balls for lunch, and pink and blue balls for dinner." "Ah, now I know what your trouble is," said the doctor. "You're not eating your greens."

Knock, knock.
– Who's there?
Marmalade.
– Marmalade who?
Marmalade me a little egg.

Knock, knock.
– Who's there?
Turnip.
– Turnip who?
Turnip this little lane, that's where I live.

Knock, knock.
– Who's there?
Jupiter.
– Jupiter who?
Jupiter fly in my soup?

Knock, knock.
– Who's there?
Stew.
– Stew who?
Stew late to ask questions.

Knock, knock.
– Who's there?
Four eggs.
– Four eggs who?
Four eggs ample.

Knock, knock.
– Who's there?
Tina.
– Tina who?
Tina pilchards.

Knock, knock.
– Who's there?
Halibut.
– Halibut who?
Halibut letting me in on the secret?

Knock, knock.
– Who's there?
Ketchup.
– Ketchup who?
Ketchup with me and I'll tell you.

Knock, knock.
– Who's there?
Pecan.
– Pecan who?
Pecan somebody your own size.

Knock, knock.
- Who's there?
Spook.
- Spook who?
Spook-etti.

Knock, knock.
- Who's there?
Cook.
- Cook who?
Cuckoo yourself! I didn't come here to be insulted.

Knock, knock.
— Who's there?
Ice cream.
— Ice cream who?
Ice cream and scream and scream until
I'm sick.

Knock, knock.
— Who's there?
Kipper.
— Kipper who?
Kipper hands to yourself.

Knock, knock.
– Who's there?
Tuna.
– Tuna who?
Tuna violin and it will sound
better.

Knock, knock.
– Who's there?
Doughnut.
– Doughnut who?
Doughnut let anyone else in but
me.

Knock, knock.
– Who's there?
Roland.
– Roland who?
Roland butter please.

Knock, knock.
– Who's there?
Watson.
– Watson who?
Watson the menu today?

Knock, knock.
– Who's there?
Egbert.
– Egbert who?
Egbert no bacon.

Knock, knock.
– Who's there?
Alec.
– Alec who?
Alec coffee but I don't like tea.

Knock, knock.
– Who's there?
Irish stew.
– Irish stew who?
Irish stew in the name of the law.

Knock, knock.
– Who's there?
Butter.
– Butter who?
Butter be quick, I need to go to the bathroom.

"Dad, do slugs taste nice?"
"Of course not – why do you ask?"
"Because you've just eaten one that was in your salad."

Did you hear about the wally who did bird impressions?
He ate worms.

"Doctor, doctor, I think I'm a dumpling."
"Now, now, don't get in a stew."

Why do Eskimos eat candles?
For light refreshment.

What's sweet and musical?
I-sing sugar.

What's the best way to get rid of
excess fat?
Divorce him.

What did the Eskimo wife sing when
her husband came home for dinner?.
"Whale Meet Again . . ."

What did the meat say when it was
about to be put on the skewer?
"Oh spear me, spear me . . ."

What is the best way to serve leftovers?
To somebody else.

What is the best way to stop rice
sticking together?
Boil each grain separately.

What did the frankfurter say to
the ketchup?
"That's enough of your sauce."

What's hot and
goes "Hoot, hoot"?
*Kentucky
Fried Owl.*

What's a hungry mathematician's food?
Anything, as long as it's a square meal.

What's yellow and deadly?
Chop sueycide.

What stays hot in the fridge?
Mustard.

What's meaty, boney and stands at an angle?
Lean chops.

What's small, blue and eats cakes?
A blue dwarf cake-eater.

What's sweet, sour, dangerous and travels?
Takeaway kung food.

What was Anne Boleyn's last meal?
Cold chops.

What's brown, round and travels at 1,000mph?
An intercontinental ballistic rissole.

What's made of pastry and is good in emergencies?
The quiche of life.

What's wrapped in tin foil and has an on/off switch?
A TV dinner.

What tree has the best food?
A pantry.

Who needs to eat a balanced diet?
A tightrope walker.

When is a red-headed idiot like a biscuit?
When he's a ginger nut.

What's black and white and comes out
of the oven spitting mad?
A hot cross nun.

What's doughy and 50 metres high?
The Leaning Tower of Pizza.

What's white one minute and
brown the next?
A white rat in a microwave.

What's brown one minute and
white the next?
A brown rat in the deep freeze.

What do you get if you cross a cow
with a pile of money?
Rich milk.

What do you get if you cross a cow
with an Arab?
A milk sheik.

What swims and gives milk?
A milk float.

What do you get if you cross a cow
with a camel?
Lumpy milkshakes.

What's the best way to stop milk
going sour?
Drink it when it's fresh.

TEACHER: Name me four things
with milk in them.
PUPIL: Coffee, tea, and two cows.

1ST CAT: How did you get on in
the milk-drinking contest?
2ND CAT: I won by six laps.

What turns without moving?
Milk – when it turns sour.

What do you get if you cross a
chicken with an octopus?
*A Sunday dinner where everybody gets a
leg.*

What do you get if you cross a
chicken with a banjo?
A self-plucking chicken.

What do you get if you cross a hen with
a tongue and a hand?
A finger-lickin' chicken.

What do you get if you cross a pig with a flea?
Pork scratchings.

What do you call a man with beef, gravy and vegetables on his head?
Stew.

What do you get if you cross a pig with an elephant?
Large pork chops.

TEACHER: What is the climate like in New Zealand?
PUPIL: Very, very cold.
TEACHER: What makes you say that?
PUPIL: Well, when they send us meat it always arrives frozen.

How do you know when you're eating rabbit stew?
When it's got hares in it.

What do you get if you cross a five pound note with a refrigerator?
Iced lolly.

What do you get if you cross a
football team with an ice cream?
Aston Vanilla.

What do you get if you cross an
idiot with a fridge?
An iced wally.

Why did the ice cream cry?
Because its mother had been a
wafer so long.

What's cold, Israeli and sells ice
cream?
Walls of Jericho.

What's the best way of making a
dead dog float?
*Take a scoop of dead dog and a
scoop of ice cream . . .*

What's the difference between an ice
cream and a bully?
You lick one, the other licks you.

What weighs half a ton, travels at
70mph and drips?
An articulated lolly.

What's orange and comes out of the
ground at 150mph?
An E-Type carrot.

What's yellow and fills fields with music?
Popcorn.

What's green and camps?
A boy sprout.

What happened when the carrot died?
There was a huge turnip at the funeral.

What do you get if the world runs out of olive oil?
Rusty olives.

What's cold and comes in tins?
Chilli beans.

What's black, sweet and makes history lessons interesting?
Dates.

What was Noah's job?
Preserving pears.

What stands on one leg and has its heart on its head?
A cabbage.

If there are two tomatoes on horseback, which one is the cowboy?
Neither – they're both redskins.

What's green, weighs a ton, and can float in a glass of Martini?
An olivephant.

What's green and for hire?
A taxi cabbage.

What are two rows of cabbages
called?
A dual cabbageway.

What's green and sings?
Elvis Parsley.

What's white on the outside, green
on the inside and jumps?
A frog sandwich.

What do you fry French food in?
Oo-la-lard.

Who invented spaghetti?
Someone using his noodle.

What's the most frightening thing in a Scottish restaurant?
A man eating haggis.

What happened when the abominable snowman ate a curry?
He melted.

What's smelly and spoken in Scotland?
Garlic.

How do people eat cheese in Wales?
Caerphilly.

What do you get if you cross a sandwich with a Parisian cathedral?
The lunchpack of Notre Dame.

What do you get if you cross a Scotsman with yellow dessert?
Tartan custard.

What do you call a Welsh biscuit?
Dai Gestive.

What do you call a Welsh apple?
Taffy apple.

Where would you find exploding spaghetti?
In the Minestrone of Defence.

What's a chicken's favourite cake?
A layer cake.

What's a lawyer's favourite pudding?
Sue-it.

What is a viper's favourite food?
Hiss fingers.

What's an astronaut's favourite meal?
Launch.

What is a frog's favourite drink?
Croaka Cola.